ANITA!

THE WOMAN BEHIND
THE BODY SHOP

I dedicate this book to the women in my life:
My mother, Ruth Older
My wife, Effin Older
My beautiful twin daughters, Amber and Willow Older
And my wife's mother, Phyllis Lawes.
—J.O.

Library of Congress Cataloging-in-Publication Data
Older, Jules.
 Anita!: the woman behind The Body Shop/by Jules
Older; illustrated by Lisa Kopper.
 p. cm.
Summary: A brief biography of the energetic woman
who founded The Body Shop with its line of cosmetics
made from natural ingredients. Includes health and
skincare advice.
 ISBN 0-88106-979-5 (reinforced for library use)
1. The Body Shop (Firm)—History—Juvenile literature.
2. Roddick, Anita, 1942- —Juvenile literature.
3. Cosmetics industry—Great Britain—History—
Juvenile literature. [1. Roddick, Anita, 1942- .
2. Businesswomen. 3. Women—Biography.
4. The Body Shop (Firm)—History.] I. Title.
HD9970.5.C674B636   1998
338.4'766855'092
[B]—dc21   97-41906
                                          CIP
                                          AC

Printed in the United States of America
(hc) 10 9 8 7 6 5 4 3 2 1

Published by Charlesbridge Publishing
85 Main Street, Watertown, MA 02172-4411
(617) 926-0329
www.charlesbridge.com

The illustrations in this book were done in
color pencil, watercolor, and ink on
Schoellershammer paper.
Photos used courtesy of The Body Shop, UK.
The display type and text type were set in
Galliard, Tekton, and Comic Strip.
Color separations were made by Eastern
Rainbow, Derry, New Hampshire
Printed and bound by Worzalla Publishing
Company, Stevens Point, Wisconsin
Production supervision
by Brian G. Walker
Designed by
Diane M. Earley
This book was printed
on recycled paper.

ANITA!

THE WOMAN BEHIND
THE BODY SHOP

Jules Older
Illustrated by Lisa Kopper

Including, at No Extra Charge,

A DOZEN THINGS YOU CAN DO FOR ANIMALS,
FOR THE WORLD, AND FOR EACH OTHER

and

FIFTEEN OF ANITA'S TIPS ON LOOKING
(AND SMELLING) YOUR BEST

and

PHOTOS FROM ANITA'S PHOTO ALBUM

as well as

THE GREATEST HITS OF THE BODY SHOP!

🌁 Charlesbridge

CHAPTER ONE
DREAMS OF GLORY

Little Anita Perella sat there—supposedly doing homework, actually daydreaming—at a table in her mother's empty café. In the kitchen, her mother was stirring a big pot of spaghetti and singing "That's Amore." Anita's mother, Gilda, was singing with an Italian accent because she grew up in Italy.

In the empty café, Anita dreamed about what she wanted to be when she grew up. It was a long dream. A lon-n-n-g dream.

"I'll be a teacher, Mum, and I'll be a lot nicer than the nuns at St. Catherine's. No, no, I'll be a famous actress, and I'll meet James Dean, and he'll fall madly in love with me! Ahh . . . . No, wait a minute, I'll become an explorer. Yes, that's it! I'll explore places nobody's ever explored before! Ooh, ooh, I've got it! I'll be a brilliant writer. That's what I'll do! Or—hold on—maybe I'll become a cool detective and catch criminals. . . ."

From the kitchen, Gilda said, "You know somethin', Anita? You're one-a crazy kid!"

Anita's Tips on Looking Your Best

TIP ONE: POTATO HEAD

If you want to find out just how clean your skin really is, slice a potato in half and wash your face with the cut side instead of a washcloth. Then look at the potato. If it's dirty, so's your face—you'd better wash more often.

CHAPTER TWO
ONE-A CRAZY KID

Anita didn't mind her mother calling her a crazy kid because she'd rather be crazy than dull.

She didn't need to worry about that! Everything she did, she did . . . differently.

Like the time Gilda took her to a talent contest at St. Catherine's School. All the other kids dressed up in their best clothes and recited a little poem or sang a little song.

Then Anita's turn came. The lights dimmed. The curtain went up. A single spotlight shone on little Anita. She didn't recite a little poem. She didn't sing a little song. She wasn't wearing her best little clothes.

Anita was wearing dirty old rags. And heavy metal chains! Instead of reciting "This Scepter'd Isle," or singing "I'm a Little Teapot," she let out one long, loud, and extremely scary scream. It sounded exactly like this:

"YAAIIIEEOWWWEEEYIIIARRRGGUHHHYAHHH!"

Gilda jumped. The whole audience jumped. Then, at the top of her little lungs, Anita bellowed a speech about how great it felt to be crazy.

As Anita took her bow, Gilda muttered, "I knew that's-a one-a crazy kid."

And Gilda was the most surprised person at the show when the principal announced, "We are pleased to award First Prize to little Anita Perella."

Anita's Tips on Looking Your Best

TIP TWO: ZIT REMOVAL

When teenagers in Rio de Janeiro get the first sign of a pimple, they sprinkle sugar on a bar of glycerin soap and wash their face with it. The soap keeps them clean, and the sugar gently sandpapers the pimple.

CHAPTER THREE
MAKEUP!

The Perella family was much too poor to afford makeup. But that didn't stop Anita. In high school, when she was in her actress phase, Anita knew she needed makeup. And she knew where to find it. Free. She used the leftovers from the café.

She smeared soot from the candles on her eyelids; that was her eye shadow.

She poured mayonnaise on her hair to make it shine.

She washed her face with potatoes instead of soap.

She painted beet juice on her lips. "That's my lipstick," Anita told her friends. "You try it."

They did try it.

Then they ate the beets.

Then they had a contest to see who had the reddest pee.

Yes, little Anita made her own cosmetics out of food. And when she got older . . . she still did!

Anita's Tips on Looking Your Best

TIP THREE: BIG HAIR CARE

If you have seriously big hair and you can't do anything with it, try using mayonnaise as a conditioner. That's right, mayonnaise. It makes even big hair shine!

CHAPTER FOUR
ON THE ROAD

After college, Anita started teaching. Anita liked teaching, but she had an itch to travel. So she applied for a summer study trip to Israel. And when the letter arrived that said "*Shalom*, Anita," Anita said, "'Bye, Mum, I'm gone!"

After Israel, Anita went to France.

After France, she went to Greece.

After Greece, she went to Switzerland.

After Switzerland, she went to Tahiti, Australia, and, finally, South Africa.

Anita didn't last long in South Africa.

Here's what happened . . . . In 1967, when she went there, white people ruled South Africa. They had passed strict laws that made it a crime for black people to eat or sleep or even live next door to whites. They said it was for the black people's own good. They said that everybody, black and white, liked the strict laws.

Anita listened politely. Then she said, in the same loud voice she'd used at her school's talent contest, "THAT IS THE BIGGEST LOAD OF RUBBISH I'VE EVER HEARD IN MY WHOLE ENTIRE LIFE! I don't pick my friends by the color of their skin, and I don't let anyone pick my friends for me. See?"

To prove her point, Anita went to a jazz club where only black people were allowed to go.

To prove *their* point, the South African police said, "Young laidy, you haav exactly 24 hours to get out of the country. Stahting r-r-right now!"

Which is why Anita came back to England in such a hurry and how

Anita
Fell
in
Love.

Anita's Tips on Looking Your Best
TIP FOUR: THE BIG ITCH

If you've been out in the sun or been eaten by bugs and your skin itches like a flea-bitten dog, take a baking soda bath. Toss two heaping tablespoons of bicarbonate of soda into the bathwater and have a long, de-itching soak.

CHAPTER FIVE
LOVE STUFF

No sooner had Anita arrived home in Littlehampton when her mom, Gilda, said, "Oooh, Anita! There's this fella you gotta meet. You're gonna love him! You'll see him tonight at my new club, the El Cubana."

That night Anita went to the El Cubana. Gordon was already there. Gilda said, "Anita, meet Gordon. Gordon, meet Anita. Ooh, I think I hear the phone ringing. I've got to go answer it."

Anita looked at Gordon.

Gordon looked at Anita.

Gilda, from behind a curtain, looked at both of them. And she sang, "When the moon hits-a your eye, Like a big pizza pie, That's amore . . ."

All that night, Gordon and Anita walked and talked.

The next day they met again, and again they walked and talked.

The next day they met again, and again they walked and talked.

The next day they met again, and again they walked and talked.

The next day they moved in together.

The next year they had a baby together. They named her Justine.

The *next* year they got married. (Even then, they didn't do things the same way as most other people.)

Here's how they got married . . .

Anita's Tips on Looking Your Best

TIP FIVE: BEATLES FOREHEAD

If you're getting pimples all over your forehead, you've probably also got a Beatles' haircut. To clear up the top of your face, lop off the hair that your mother always complains about. Not only will it make her happy, but it will keep the oils in your hair from building bumps on that pretty forehead of yours.

CHAPTER SIX
HOW THEY GOT MARRIED

One day Anita said, "Gordon, I have something to tell you."

She paused dramatically. "I'm pregnant! We're going to have another baby!"

She paused again, even more dramatically. "Gordon, let's go on a trip. To celebrate. We'll go to the United States. To San Francisco. To see our hippie friends."

She paused to see if Gordon had passed out. "And we'll take Justine—she's fifteen months old, almost, and the travel will broaden her horizons. We'll just buy a pack, and I'll carry her on my back. Let's do it, Gordon, let's go!"

And that's just what they did. They flew Last-Class.

One day Gordon and Anita and Justine and their hippie friends drove to Reno, Nevada. Reno is famous for three things:

1. Big-time gambling.
2. Quick divorces.
3. Even quicker marriages.

Gordon and Anita couldn't gamble—they had no money.

They couldn't divorce—they weren't married.

This left only two options:

A. Leave town.

B. Scrape together $25, borrow a ring from their hippie friends, and get hitched.

They chose Option B. For her wedding, Anita wore tattered corduroy pants, a red rain slicker, and old sneakers. Her big belly stuck way out in front while Justine howled and hiccuped on her back.

The bride looked luvly, just luvly.

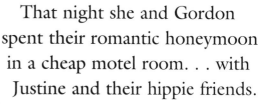

That night she and Gordon spent their romantic honeymoon in a cheap motel room. . . with Justine and their hippie friends. Then they came back to Littlehampton, had a second little girl, whom they named Samantha, and bought a little old hotel. They worked day & night and night & day in the hotel. Then they opened a restaurant. They worked day & night and night & day in the hotel and restaurant.

When they ran out of days & nights and nights & days, they sold the restaurant. Which turned out to be just as well in light of

. . . Gordon's Secret Desire.

Anita's Tips on Looking Your Best

TIP SIX: DON'T GET BURNED!

If you do it right, the sun will give you a nice healthy-looking tan. If you do it wrong, it will burn you. Not only does burning hurt you, it hurts your skin. To avoid sunburn, use sunblock. It will let you tan; it won't let you burn, at least if you follow the directions and generally use your noggin.

Ten-year-old Anita.

Anita backpacking in the
Middle East in 1963.

Working at the
UN in Geneva.

On the beach back home
in Littlehampton in 1969.

Anita with her second
child, Sam, in 1972.

The first shop!

Bottling.

At the shop in
the late '70's.

Anita in one of her many stores.

©Thomas L. Kelly

Photo by Sue Adler.

Anita receiving one of her many
awards, the Veuve-Clicquot Award.

CHAPTER SEVEN
GORDON'S SECRET DESIRE

One night Gordon said, "Anita, there's something I very much want to do."

"What is it, love?"

"I've wanted to do it for years and years."

"What is it, love?"

"You could say it's my secret desire."

"What *is* it, love?"

"I . . . er . . . um . . ."

"Yes?"

"I want to go on a horse ride."

"A horse ride? Well, that's fine, love. Will you be back in time for lunch?"

Gordon shook his head.

"For dinner?"

Gordon shook his head.

"So you'll just be gone overnight?"

Gordon shook his head.

"A couple of days? A week?"

Gordon shook his head.

Anita's voice grew quiet. "A month? A whole month?"

Gordon shook his head. "Two years, Anita. I want to ride a horse from Buenos Aires, Argentina, to New York, U.S.A."

When Anita came to, she said . . .

Well, what would *you* say when you came to? What would you say if your husband announced that he wanted to leave you and your two young daughters and an old hotel and almost no money for two years so he could ride a horse from Argentina to New York?

Here's what Anita said: "Well, love, if that's your secret desire, you'd better do it. And we'd better think of something for me to do on my own while you're gone. Something that will leave me more time for the children. Something that will earn us money."

"What would you like, Anita? Whatever it is, I'll help you in every way."

"Oh, I don't know . . ." Anita thought for a moment. "Maybe a little shop."

Anita's Tips on Looking Your Best

TIP SEVEN: DON'T DIE FROM DYE

If you must dye your hair, take this tip from me. Dye is bad for your skin and probably bad for your health. It also looks a little strange on your forehead. So before you apply it, spread Vitamin E cream all around your hairline to keep your skin from turning into the new color of your hair.

EXTREMELY ANNOYING

 The next day Anita told her mother about Gordon's trip and about wanting to open a little shop. Gilda looked at her and said, "What are you gonna sell in this little shop?"

 "Cosmetics."

 "Cosmetics? What's cosmetics?"

 "You know, shampoo and perfume and face cream—things like that."

"Honey," Gilda said, "there's an awful lot of cosmetics shops around already."

"Yes, but I find them all extremely annoying."

"Why?"

"Well, for one thing, they only sell one size of everything. If I want to try something new, I have to buy a big bottle. Then, if I don't like it, I can't return it." Anita sounded extremely annoyed.

"Hmmm. OK, so what else?"

"Well, a lot of the time I think I'm paying more for some fancy container than the stuff it contains. Boy, does that make me mad!" Anita was turning red.

"Calm down, honey."

"No, there's more! Most of these companies test their cosmetics on animals. A lot of the time they hurt the animals or even kill them. That's disgusting. Disgusting, disgusting, disgusting!" Anita turned redder.

"You're getting overexcited, Anita. Take a deep breath. Calm yourself."

"I am calm. I have never been calmer. I am the very picture of calm. But, listen to this! A lot of the stuff you buy comes right out of a chemistry set. It's all chemicals! This might sound crazy, Mum, but I want to sell cosmetics with natural ingredients."

"Natural ingredients?"

"Yes, natural ingredients. Like . . . well, like cocoa butter. In Tahiti, the women rub cocoa butter all over themselves. It keeps their skin soft and smooth. I want to sell natural stuff like that. Do you think I'm crazy, Mum?"

Gilda looked at her daughter for a long time. Then she sighed and said, "Honey, this time I think you're one-a smart cookie! You feeling better now?"

The very next day Anita set off to find a little shop. It had to be cheap.

She found a little shop in Brighton. It was *very* cheap. The roof leaked, the floor sagged, and nobody had rented it for a long, long time. Maybe because the insides were covered with. . . . Here's a hint—it smells and it's green.

Anita's Tips on Looking Your Best

TIP EIGHT: SMELLING GOOD! (PART ONE)

Here's one of the potentially embarrassing things about being human—people can smell you more than you can smell yourself. It's potentially embarrassing because we humans can smell awful if we don't keep ourselves clean. Here's one thing you can do to avoid smelling awful: Wash a lot, at least once a day, with mild soap and water. Turn your armpits into charmpits.

CHAPTER NINE
CEASE AND DESIST!

Besides a leaking roof and a sagging floor, the little shop in Brighton had one more charming feature. It had mold.

Mold is a fungus that grows in dark, damp places . . . places like shops with leaking roofs. Two other things you should know about mold are:

A. It smells.

B. It's green.

Anita scraped and sprayed and cleaned, trying to get rid of that mold. But no matter what she did, she could not get rid of:

A. The smell.

B. The green.

Finally, she had a bright idea. "I know!" she announced to herself, as she scrubbed the foul green walls for the hundred and eleventh time. "I know! I'll cover this yucky smell with wonderful smells of flowers and perfumes. And I'll cover this icky green mold with pretty green paint."

That is why every branch of The Body Shop all over the world smells so sweet . . . and why each one is painted green!

After painting till her arms were sore, Anita was finally ready to open for business. On Saturday, March 27, 1976, at exactly nine o'clock in the morning, Anita unlocked the little front door of her little shop and put up a big sign that said in bright gold letters: THE BODY SHOP.

Now this may sound innocent enough, but as things turned out, it wasn't.

Before a day had passed, she got a letter from a lawyer. The letter said something like this: "Kindly cease and desist from advertising, promoting, or in any way whatsoever describing your emporium as The Body Shop."

Translated into English, this means, "TAKE DOWN THE BLASTED SIGN, ANITA!"

Why did the lawyer send Anita this letter? Because he was working for two other businesses very near her store.

And why didn't the two businesses very near her store want a sign out front that said "The Body Shop"? Because the two businesses very near her store were . . . can you guess?

Because the businesses very near her store were undertakers!

Anita—always calm, always reasonable—said, "Stuff 'em—the sign stays!"

Just to make sure it stayed, she called the newspaper and told them about these mean undertakers ganging up on some poor (that part was true), defenseless (that part wasn't) woman who was trying to feed her children while her husband rode a horse across South America.

The paper printed the story.

The sign stayed.

Anita's Tips on Looking Your Best

TIP NINE: SMELLING GOOD! (PART TWO)

Here's a second thing you can do to avoid smelling: Wash your clothes, too. A lot of the time, the smell is in your clothes, not on your skin. So keep your clothes as clean as your body, and keep your body as clean as falling snow.

CHAPTER TEN
THE SCENT OF A WOMAN

It's one thing to buy a moldy old shop and turn it into something nice. It's another thing to make all the stuff you're going to sell in that shop. But that's what Anita had to do.

She knew what she wanted, but not how to get it. When she called the suppliers who sold the ingredients for cosmetics, the conversation went like this:

Anita: I'm opening a new shop, and I need some ingredients.

Supplier: That's what we're here for.

Anita: Good. I'd like three gallons of cocoa butter and one gal—

Supplier: What? What's cocoa butter?

Anita: It's what I need three gallons of.

Supplier: Lady, are you a chocolate shop?

Anita: No, I'm a cosmetics shop.

Supplier: Then you must be cracked. Like a coconut! People *eat* cocoa—they don't smear it on their face!

Anita: (heavy sigh)

Finally, Anita phoned an herbalist. Now the conversation went like this:

Anita: You don't, by the remotest chance, have cocoa butter, do you?

Herbalist: Certainly, Madame. Cocoa butter and jojoba oil and almond oil and aloe vera and strawberry oil and—

Anita: And I'll be right over!

Three gallons !!

Anita spent that night, and the next night, and the next night mixing up big batches of cocoa butter and jojoba oil and almond oil and aloe vera and twenty other natural ingredients. When her arms were too tired to mix any more, she hauled them over to her new, green shop.

Then Anita took oil of strawberry and sprinkled it all over the pavement. And she poured strawberry oil over the front of her store.

She thought, "People will smell that delicious smell, and they'll follow it right into my shop. Am I clever, or what!"

She was clever, all right—the people came! And they found that Anita had turned the wet and dirty building into a country store filled with dried flowers and delicious smells. Along the walls were twenty-five different cosmetics in five different sizes of plain bottles. The bottles were filled with cosmetics made from honey and oatmeal, cucumber and seaweed, avocado and hawthorn, and, yes, cocoa butter! The customers bought them all.

Pretty soon Anita wanted to open another store of The Body Shop. With some help, that's just what she did.

poo!

stinky!

Anita's Tips on Looking Your Best

TIP TEN: SMELLING GOOD! (PART THREE)

Here's the third thing you can do to avoid smelling awful: If you've washed your body and washed your clothes, and you still smell, either start using a deodorant or stop eating meat. Or both. And by the way, if a friend tells you that you smell, don't get mad, get clean. It takes a good friend to tell you the embarrassing truth.

CHAPTER ELEVEN
BAD NEWS, GOOD NEWS

Meanwhile, back in South America, Gordon was riding his horse. He rode through Argentina. He rode through Peru. He'd ridden halfway through Bolivia when something terrible happened. Something *really* terrible.

Gordon's horse fell over a cliff and died.

Gordon and the horse were pals. They'd been together for 2,000 miles. When the horse died, Gordon flew back to Littlehampton.

Gordon kissed Justine. He kissed Samantha. He kissed Gilda. He kissed Anita. He kissed Anita again. He asked her, "What can I do to help?"

Anita looked at him with love in her eyes. She answered,

"Bottling."

Bottling. Anita hated bottling. It meant pouring Honey & Oatmeal Scrub Mask and Seaweed & Birch Shampoo and Cucumber Cleansing Milk and Avocado Moisture Cream and Hawthorn Hand Cream and Cocoa Butter Body Lotion and a whole lot of other stuff from five-gallon containers into five different sizes of plastic bottles and tubs. She was sick and tired of it.

"Gordon, I'm sick and tired of it!" she said. "Will you do it for me?"

Gordon said only three words: "As. You. Wish."

Anita's Tips on Looking Your Best

TIP ELEVEN: SAVE YOUR LIFE, YOUR SKIN, AND YOUR MONEY, ALL AT THE SAME TIME . . .

Don't smoke.

CHAPTER TWELVE

R-I-C-H!

By working day & night and night & day, and by working full-time & overtime & daylight saving time & Greenwich mean time, Anita and Gordon and the people who worked with them made the two stores of The Body Shop a rip-roaring success.

So they opened another branch of The Body Shop. And another. And another.

All of a sudden, there were shops in England and Belgium and Iceland and Denmark and Greece and Canada and—there were a lot of shops.

And, for the first time in her life, Anita found she was . . . r-i-c-h!

She opened a bottle of champagne. She took a deep breath. She said, "Let's use the money to make the world a better place."

And that's just what she did. The Body Shop started by helping Greenpeace. Greenpeace is a group that protects the seas from people who dump poisons in them and protects whales from people who want to slaughter them.

The Body Shop helped Friends of the Earth, a group that protects the earth from people who dump poisons in the air, in the earth, and in the water.

The Body Shop helped Cultural Survival, a group that protects the tribes who live in the rain forest from people who want to chase them out and chop the forest down.

The Body Shop helped sign up a thousand new members to Amnesty International, a group that protects people who get locked up simply because of the things they believe in.

Why did they do all this? Why do they still do it? Because Anita believes that businesses have to give something back to the world.

Anita's Tips on Looking Your Best

TIP TWELVE: SMOKING (PART TWO)

About the worst thing you can do to your skin and body is to smoke. It will make your skin wrinkle and take energy away from your body. The energy part means this: However fast you run, high you jump, or long you can dance if you smoke, you can go faster, higher, and longer if you don't. So don't.

CHAPTER THIRTEEN
THE RAIN IN SPAIN

The Body Shop was a success. The company that started with one little shop in Brighton became one of Great Britain's biggest exporters. That means they sold more stuff overseas than almost any other company.

That's why the queen of England sent Anita this letter stamped with the royal seal: "Her Royal Majesty is pleased to inform you that you have been admitted to the Order of the British Empire.

"Yoiks!" Anita shouted. "They're giving me an OBE!"

Justine said, "Then we'll have to get you some new clothes for when the queen hands you your medal."

Samantha said, "I s'pose you're going to accept this meaningless gesture from an obsolete and archaic monarchy."

Anita said, "Too right I am! C'mon you two—let's buy Momma a new dress!"

With her daughters' help, Anita got the right dress for the ceremony . . . but that's the only thing she got right. Her trouble started with hats.

"Sorry, Mum," Justine said, "but you've got to have a hat as well. Women are expected to wear hats when they meet the queen of England."

"Why?" Anita asked.

"Why? I'll tell you why," Sam shouted. "So they can show the world that they're lackeys to the patriarchal, imperialist, monarchist—"

"Thank you, darling," Anita said, "And thank you for your fashion advice, Justine. But I'm not wearing a hat. I look daft in hats."

Justine sighed. "But, Mum—"

"No *buts*. And no hats, either!"

Anita's Tips on Looking Your Best

TIP THIRTEEN: BEAUTY REST

One of the best ways to maintain the luster of the skin is to let it rest. Beauty rest is well named. For a good night's sleep, try a late-night banana snack. Bananas are a natural relaxant because they contain the sleep-inducing amino acid tryptophan.

CHAPTER FOURTEEN
THE QUEEN AND I

When she reached the huge auditorium, Anita quickly observed that she was the only woman in the entire hall who was *sans chapeau*—hatless. She began to worry that she should have listened to Justine.

Just then, a very well-dressed man said, "Please, may I have your complete attention? I am here to instruct you on how to act in the presence of the queen."

The group grew quiet. "Thank you," said the well-dressed (but 'atless) man. "One by one, you are to walk slowly—*slowly*—down the carpet to where Her Majesty is seated. When you reach Her Royal Majesty . . . Mrs. Roddick, are you listening?"

"Yes. Yes. Sorry." Anita was muttering to herself about hats.

"Thank you. When you reach Her Royal Majesty, you stop and curtsy."

Anita practiced a curtsy.

"Very nice, Mrs. Roddick. Once you've curtsied, the queen might ask you a brief question, and if so, you may respond with a brief answer. Please be brief"—here he looked hard at Anita—"Her Majesty has many people to honor today."

Anita smiled an "I'll be brief" smile.

The man continued: "Once the brief pleasantries have been concluded, Her Majesty will hand you your medal and shake your hand. Once she does that, you curtsy again. Finally, you turn left and walk out of the auditorium. Now, is that clear?"

Anita wanted to say, "'Scuse me? Would you go over that one more time?" But just then, the well-dressed man turned to her and said, "Mrs. Roddick, it's your turn."

Anita took her first step down the aisle. "Right," she murmured, "I'm off."

She walked up to the queen. She curtsied. She didn't fall down. "Why, this isn't so hard," she thought. "What was I so worried about?"

"And how are your projects going in America, Mrs. Roddick?" the queen asked.

Big mistake, Queen.

"Oh, very well, Your Majesty, very well, indeed. Y'see we're opening this huge factory in North Carolina—well, when I say huge, I mean the size of a dozen football fields, well, maybe ten football fields, oh, let's call it eleven football fields, the place is going to be big. Anyway, it's in North Carolina—that's south of Washington, you know, and north of . . . let's see, is it north of Miami? Yes, it's definitely north of Miami and—"

"Ahem."

The "ahem" wasn't very loud, but it was right by Anita's ear. It was the kind of "ahem" that, even if it weren't right by your ear and even if it weren't said by the well-dressed man who had suddenly appeared right by your ear, would stop you dead in your tracks.

Which is just what it did to Anita's story.

The well-dressed man smiled at Anita. His smile said "Stop. Talking. Now." With the tiniest nod of his head, he pointed toward the door.

"Right, then, Your Majesty," Anita said, "I'll just be going." With that, she turned around and marched down the aisle and out the door.

Gilda and Gordon and Justine and Sam were all waiting for her. "Well?" they asked. *"Well?"*

"Well . . . I'll admit I had a rocky moment or two, but in the end, I got it right. I met the queen and collected my medal, and that's that. Let's go to lunch—I'm starving."

"So where's-a the medal?" Gilda asked.

Anita went white. She went red. She went purple. She suddenly remembered three things. She'd gone out the wrong way. She'd forgotten to curtsy on her way out. And she'd forgotten— yes, it's true—she'd forgotten to get the bloomin' medal!

Anita's Tips on Looking Your Best

TIP FOURTEEN: NATURAL TOOTHPASTE

Run out of toothpaste? Try these natural substitutes: Slices of fresh strawberry rubbed over teeth remove most stains. Lemon peel rubbed over the teeth removes brown stains. Rinse after rubbing. For fresh breath, try chewing parsley or watercress.

LAST CHAPTER
THE MINISTER OF SURPRISES

When Anita was little, she wanted to be everything when she grew up.

Now when you ask Anita what she wants to be when she grows up, she says, "I want to be the Minister of Surprises."

Well, she started with one store of The Body Shop, and now there are more than 1,500.

She opened one little shop in a little town in England, and now there are shops in more than forty-six countries.

She began life in a poor Italian family, and now she's the Big Cheese of a huge international company.

She used to make cosmetics out of food . . . and she still makes cosmetics out of food. (And out of other things, too.)

Anita's Tips on Looking Your Best

TIP FIFTEEN: NAILS!

If you want to have good, strong nails, try this: Three times a day drink a glass of water containing one tablespoon of cider vinegar or pure lemon juice. Or use the same mixture as a hand bath.

She started out with strong ideals—she wanted to help make the world a better place. Now she and the staff of The Body Shop all over the world still help make the world a better place.

Anita wants to be the Minister of Surprises?

Some people think she already is.

A DOZEN THINGS YOU CAN DO FOR ANIMALS, FOR THE WORLD, AND FOR EACH OTHER

1. Plant a tree. But before you dig the hole, picture how it's going to look when it grows up—otherwise you might be in for a surprise.

2. Plant one hundred sunflower seeds in unexpected places.

3. When you brush your teeth, turn off the water between rinses. This saves the world a lot of water.

4. When you're among friends, don't flush the toilet every time you pee. Every time you don't flush, you save gallons of water.

5. Help keep the world clean—pick up other people's litter. And if they see *you* picking up *their* mess, they may feel so bad that the next time, they won't litter again!

6. Walk, run, hop, skip, bike, roller-skate, inline skate, ski—do anything except ride in a car for short trips.

7. Bus, train, trolley, subway—use public transportation instead of a car for medium trips.

8. Share rides with friends for long trips. (Don't use two or three cars when one will do.)

9. Don't drop plastic soda-can loops on the ground. Animals can swallow them and get hurt. Smaller animals can get them caught around their necks and choke.

10. If you see somebody playing with matches, tell them to stop. Forest fires really hurt animals.

11. Help someone with their homework.

12. Say something nice to somebody every day. Remember—it's nice to be important, but it's more important to be nice!

THE GREATEST HITS

April 27, 1942—Gordon Roddick is born in Aran, Scotland.

October 23, 1942—Anita Perella is born in Littlehampton, England.

1962—Anita goes to live and work in Israel. Then she goes on to France, Greece, and Switzerland.

1964—Anita starts teaching eleven- to fourteen-year-olds at Maude Allen Secondary Modern School for Girls in Littlehampton. This is the same school she attended when she was eleven to fourteen.

1967 (A Big Year)—Anita goes to Tahiti, Australia, Madagascar, Mauritius, and South Africa. Anita and Gordon meet and instantly fall in love!

August 8, 1969—Justine is born.

December 3, 1970—Gordon and Anita get married in Reno, Nevada, U.S.A. with a borrowed ring.

July 1, 1971—Samantha is born. Gordon and Anita buy St. Winifred's Hotel in Littlehampton.

September, 1975—Gordon announces that he wants to go horseback riding. For two years.

Saturday, March 27, 1976, 9 a.m.—The first branch of The Body Shop opens its strawberry-soaked front door in Brighton, England.

OF THE BODY SHOP!

 1978—The first branch of The Body Shop outside the United Kingdom opens in a store the size of a closet in Brussels, Belgium.

 1979—Sweden and Greece get The Body Shop.

 1980—The Body Shop comes to Canada. There are now eighteen shops in the United Kingdom and six overseas.

 April, 1984—The Body Shop is launched on the stock market. Anita and Gordon are instant millionaires. Anita wins the Veuve Clicquot Business Woman of the Year Award.

 1985—Greenpeace posters go up in The Body Shop.

 1987—The Body Shop wins the Company of the Year Award from the Confederation of British Businesses.

 July 1, 1988—The first branch of The Body Shop in the United States opens in New Yawk City.

1988—Anita gets an OBE. Without a hat. Anita also wins the Retailer of the Year Award.

 1989—The Body Shop comes to New Zealand and Gibraltar. Now there are 139 shops in the United Kingdom and 315 overseas! Anita wins the Marketing Society Award and the United Nations Global 500 Award.

 1990—Tokyo, Japan, gets The Body Shop. And the International Women's Forum names Anita "The Year's Woman Who Has Made a Difference."

GREATEST HITS!

 1991—Anita's autobiography, *Body & Soul,* is published in ten languages.

 1993—The thousandth branch of The Body Shop opens in Madrid. The company campaigns in support of writer Ken Saro-Wiwa, persecuted by the Nigerian government. The Body Shop also supports payments to the Ogoni people of Nigeria for damage caused by oil companies.

 1994—The Body Shop campaigns against domestic violence. The company makes information available to its employees and customers so that they will know what to do if they don't feel safe from harm at home.

The company also sails into cyberspace at http://www.the-body-shop.com.

 1995—Ken Saro-Wiwa and eight other Ogoni activists are executed by Nigeria's dictatorship—The Body Shop leads the worldwide outrage in protest of the murders.

 1996—Happy Twentieth Birthday to The Body Shop! The company celebrates by launching its biggest-ever campaign to ban animal testing in Europe.

November 1996—The Body Shop collects more than four million signatures on a petition to ban animal testing!

 1997—The Body Shop creates a new poster girl—Ruby, size 18 and proud of it! Her motto? "There are three billion women who don't look like supermodels and only eight who do. Love your body."

To be continued...

THE END